CONTENTS

Using this guide... 4
Route summary table ... 6
Map key ... 7
Introduction ... 9
   Walking northern Perthshire ... 10
   When to visit ... 10
   Travel ... 10
   Accommodation and food ... 11
   Special places to see ... 12

The walks

1.	The Falls of Bruar	13
2.	Glen Tilt and Blair Castle	17
3.	South Loch Rannoch Forest Trail	23
4.	Allean Forest Trail	27
5.	Loch Faskally and Pitlochry salmon ladder	31
6.	Ben Vrackie	37
7.	Black Spout and two distilleries	43
8.	Inver Path and Pine Cone Point	49
9.	The Braan and Inchewan paths	55
10.	Birnam Hill	61
11.	From Aberfeldy to Grandtully along the Tay	67
12.	The Birks of Aberfeldy	73
13.	Aberfeldy bridges, St David's Well and Castle Menzies	77
14.	The Falls of Acharn	83
15.	Drummond Hill and Black Rock Viewpoint	89

Useful information ... 94

USING THIS GUIDE

Routes in this book

In this book you will find a selection of easy or moderate walks suitable for almost everyone, including casual walkers and families with children, or for when you only have a short time to fill. The routes have been carefully chosen to allow you to explore the area and its attractions. Most routes are circular or out-and-back, although some linear walks may be included that use public transport to get back to the start. Although there may be some climbs there is no challenging terrain, but do bear in mind that conditions can sometimes be wet or muddy underfoot. A route summary table is included on page 6 to help you choose the right walk.

Clothing and footwear

You won't need any special equipment to enjoy these walks. The weather in Britain can be changeable, so choose clothing suitable for the season and wear or carry a waterproof jacket. For footwear, comfortable walking boots or trainers with a good grip are best. A small rucksack for drinks, snacks and spare clothing is useful. See www.adventuresmart.uk.

Walk descriptions

At the beginning of each walk you'll find all the information you need:

- start/finish location, with a what3words address to help you find it
- parking and transport information, estimated walking time, total distance and climb
- details of public toilets available along the route and where you can get refreshments
- a summary of the key highlights of the walk and what you might see

Timings given are the time to complete the walk at a reasonable walking pace. Allow extra time for extended stops or if walking with children.

The route is described in clear, easy-to-follow directions, with each waypoint marked on an accompanying map extract. It's a good idea to read the whole of the route instructions before setting out, so that you know what to expect.

Maps, GPX files and what3words

Extracts from the OS® 1:25,000 map accompany each route. GPX files for all the walks in this book are available to download at www.cicerone.co.uk/1252/gpx.

What3words is a free smartphone app which identifies every 3m square of the globe with a unique three-word address, e.g. ///destiny.cafe.sonic. For more information see https://what3words.com/products/what3words-app.

SHORT WALKS PERTHSHIRE NORTH

PITLOCHRY, ABERFELDY AND DUNKELD

by Nicole Bukaty

Wide tracks make for comfortable walking to the viewpoint (Walk 15)

USING THIS GUIDE

Walking with children

Even young children can be surprisingly strong walkers, but every family is different and you may need to adapt the timings given in this book to take that into account. Make sure you go at the pace of the slowest member and choose a walk with an exciting objective in mind, such as a cave, river, waterfall or picnic spot. Many of the walks can be shortened to suit – suggestions are included at the end of the route description.

Dogs

Sheep or cattle may be found grazing on a number of these walks. Keep dogs under control at all times so that they don't scare or disturb livestock or wildlife. Cattle, particularly cows with calves, may occasionally pose a risk to walkers with dogs. If you ever feel threatened by cattle, let go of your dog's lead and let it run free. Always bag and bin dog poo, or take it home.

Enjoying the countryside responsibly

Enjoy the countryside and treat it with respect to protect our natural environments. In Scotland, you can enjoy the outdoors on most land and inland water, as long as you act responsibly and follow the Scottish Outdoor Access Code – www.outdooraccess-scotland.scot.

The Scottish Outdoor Access Code

Responsible access can be enjoyed over most of Scotland including parks, hills, moors, mountains and woods, beaches and the coast, lochs, rivers and canals, and some areas of farmland. The key principles are:

Take responsibility for your own actions

- park sensibly and do not create an obstruction
- take your rubbish home

Respect the interests of other people

- respect the needs of other people enjoying or working in the outdoors
- follow any reasonable advice from land managers
- on farmland, leave gates as you find them and keep to unsown ground, field edges or paths
- access rights do not usually apply to farmyards, but if a well-used path goes through a farmyard, you can follow it
- paths are shared with others – let people know you are coming so you do not alarm them, and slow down, stop or stand aside if needed

Care for the environment

- don't disturb or damage wildlife or historic places
- never light open fires, barbecues or fire bowls in dry periods or near to forests, farmland, buildings or historic sites at any time
- never cut down or damage trees

ROUTE SUMMARY TABLE

WALK NAME	START POINT	TIME	DISTANCE
1. The Falls of Bruar	House of Bruar car park	1hr	2.7km (1.7 miles)
2. Glen Tilt and Blair Castle	Glen Tilt car park, Blair Atholl	3hr	8.5km (5.3 miles)
3. South Loch Rannoch Forest Trail	Loch Rannoch Forest car park	2hr 30min	8.3km (5.2 miles)
4. Allean Forest Trail	Allean Forest car park	1hr 30min	4km (2.5 miles)
5. Loch Faskally and Pitlochry salmon ladder	Pitlochry high street	2hr	5.2km (3.2 miles)
6. Ben Vrackie	Ben Vrackie car park	4hr 30min	8.6km (5.3 miles)
7. Black Spout and two distilleries	Pitlochry high street	2hr	6.5km (4 miles)
8. Inver Path and Pine Cone Point	The Hermitage car park	3hr	10.8km (6.7 miles)
9. The Braan and Inchewan paths	The Hermitage car park	3hr	10.2km (6.3 miles)
10. Birnam Hill	Dunkeld Cathedral	3hr 15min	8.5km (5.3 miles)
11. From Aberfeldy to Grandtully along the Tay	The Birks Cinema, Aberfeldy	2hr 30min	8km (5 miles)
12. The Birks of Aberfeldy	Birks of Aberfeldy car park	1hr 45min	3.5km (2.2 miles)
13. Aberfeldy bridges, St David's Well and Castle Menzies	The Birks Cinema, Aberfeldy	2hr 30min	6.9km (4.3 miles)
14. The Falls of Acharn	Falls of Acharn car park	2hr 30min	5.5km (3.4 miles)
15. Drummond Hill and Black Rock Viewpoint	Kenmore Beach	2hr 30min	8.8km (5.5 miles)

ROUTE SUMMARY TABLE

HIGHLIGHTS
Waterfalls and stone bridges
Rolling countryside, great views, castle and gardens
Native Caledonian forest and a forest loch
Remains of a Clachan community and Iron Age ring fort
Suspension bridge, scenic loch, fish ladder and hydroelectric dam
Summit views to the Highlands and over Pitlochry
Quaint village, 60m-waterfall and two distilleries
The Tay river and a pine cone-shaped viewpoint
The Hermitage, Rumbling Bridge and Birnam Woods
Cathedral, views from King's Seat hill summit and a quarry
Linear walk along a disused railway and a section of the Rob Roy Way
Poetical waterfalls and Robert Burns connection
Historical and modern bridges, a Celtic well and a castle
Waterfalls, hermit's cave, views to mountains and a stone circle
Forests and views over Loch Tay, Kenmore and mountain

SYMBOLS USED ON ROUTE MAPS

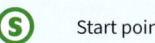 Start point

 Finish point

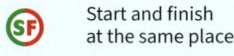 Start and finish at the same place

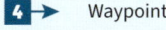 Waypoint

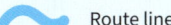 Route line

MAPPING IS SHOWN AT A SCALE OF 1:25,000

```
0 KM      0.25      0.5
0 miles        0.25
```

DOWNLOAD THE GPX FILES FOR FREE AT
www.cicerone.co.uk/1252/gpx

The Tay is Scotland's longest river flowing for 188km, almost entirely in Perthshire (Walk 10)

INTRODUCTION

Perthshire is the 'gateway to the Highlands'

Perthshire lies in the heart of Scotland and is a wonderful destination for scenic walking, offering fascinating history woven into a mosaic of landscapes. Divided by the Highland Boundary Fault, it is a land of contrasts: tranquil arable countryside in the south and superb rugged mountains in its north. Perthshire's northern territory is exceptional; it is rightly deemed the gateway to the Scottish Highlands. The region's magnificent large lochs follow the east–west fault line axis, creating spectacular glens, with waterfalls tumbling at every turn, while on the slopes extensive reforestations, spearheaded in the 18th century, intertwine with protected native woodland and soaring heritage trees.

Northern Perthshire's rich history is narrated in its Bronze Age monuments, Pictish stones, medieval ruins, and fairy-tale style castles. The Tay, Scotland's longest river, has been a communication route since time immemorial, with charming towns and villages sprinkled along its banks. The mid 18th-century arrival of the railway placed the area firmly on the map, transforming it into a desirable place to live, and attracting noble visitors who succumbed to its romantically wild allure.

Walking northern Perthshire

This guidebook explores special locations in northern Perthshire that are cherished by locals and visitors alike. All the walks are accessible at any time of year, although in winter Walk 6 (Ben Vrackie) may be too challenging and could require special equipment. Overall, the routes involve some uphill walking but are well signed and mainly follow tracks and footpaths. All the walks are circular or there-and-back routes, apart from Walk 11 which is a linear walk using a bus to return to the start.

In spring, bluebells carpet the forests between Aberfeldy and Kenmore

When to visit

March officially marks the start of springtime in Perthshire, bringing brighter and more predictable weather, and daffodils and bluebells pepper the landscape. Summer has its lovely long hours of daylight but can bring a lot of rain. Autumn is a lovely time to visit and the colours are spectacular along all the walks, particularly in late October and early November. Wintertime brings shorter days and unpredictable stormy weather, but also awe-inspiring views of snow-capped mountains, star-filled skies and mesmerising northern lights. Generally, May, June and September see the least rain but it is best to always bring waterproofs for trips to Perthshire.

Travel

Public transport runs infrequently in northern Perthshire, and timetables and frequency differ in winter (1 November to 31 March). Therefore, most visitors rely on a car, taking advantage of the key A9 arterial road along which are the settlements of Dunkeld (Walks 8–10), Birnam, Pitlochry (Walks 5–7) and Blair Atholl (Walk 2). B roads and local roads link to all other walks in this guidebook.

Dunkeld and Birnam, Pitlochry and Blair Atholl have train stations with links to Edinburgh, Glasgow and

ACCOMMODATION AND FOOD

Highland 'coos' at Atholl estate (Walk 2)

Inverness. For railway information see www.scotrail.co.uk.

Citylink (www.citylink.co.uk) bus number M91 runs daily, once up, then down the A9 between Edinburgh and Inverness, calling at Birnam, Blair Atholl and House of Bruar. Visit https://uk.megabus.com for further coach options from major cities. For schedules for local bus routes, visit www.pkc.gov.uk/article/14961/Highland-Perthshire-and-Stanley-area-timetables, particularly useful for Walks 1, 3, 4, 11, 12, 13, 14 and 15.

For cyclists and bikepackers, Acharn, Kenmore, Aberfeldy, Pitlochry, Blair Atholl and House of Bruar are interconnected by National Cycle Route 7, and Route 77 connects to Dunkeld and Birnam. See www.sustrans.org.uk/national-cycle-network.

Accommodation and food

Wild camping is legal in Scotland, but ensure you respect the Scottish Outdoor Access Code (www.outdooraccess-scotland.scot/practical-guide-all/camping).

The best bases for a wide choice of accommodation options are Pitlochry, Dunkeld, Aberfeldy, Kenmore and Blair Atholl. Pitlochry, Dunkeld, Birnam and Aberfeldy have many cafes and restaurants; Kenmore also has options, although opening times vary

Taymouth Castle's gate house on the A827 between Kenmore and Aberfeldy

seasonally. Blair Atholl has an option at its namesake hotel, as do Kinloch Rannoch and House of Bruar. There is nowhere to eat in Acharn itself.

Special places to see

A fantastic stop along the A9 is the visitor centre at the Pass of Killicrankie where the Battle of Killiecrankie on 27 July 1689 saw the first Jacobite uprising and defeat of the governmental army. Killicrankie's 1864 viaduct is beautiful with its ten arches and crenellated parapets. For adrenaline-seekers, the first and only fixed bungee-jumping platform in Britain is located here.

Driving from Pitlochry to Kenmore along the A827, take a swift detour between Grandtully and Aberfeldy to visit St Mary's Church; built in 1533, it has one of only two original painted church ceilings in Scotland from the period.

Croft Moraig Stone Circle, a double stone circle estimated to date from 3000 to 2000BC, is visible from the A827 between Aberfeldy and Kenmore. Once in Kenmore, venture into the grounds of monumental Taymouth Castle, or visit the Scottish Crannog Centre nearby, with ancient artefacts and a replica Iron Age village.

After Walk 3, continue along Loch Rannoch, then west along the B846 to reach remote Rannoch train station and its quaint tearoom (closed in winter). Finally, drive through marvellous Glen Lyon, Scotland's longest and most remote glen. On your way, a little further along the B846 from Weem, stop for a photo at the road sign in the hamlet of Dull, humorously twinned with Boring in the USA and Bland in Australia.

WALK 1
The Falls of Bruar

Start/finish	*House of Bruar car park*
Locate	*///tastier.prompts.dogs*
Cafes/pubs	*House of Bruar foodhall and cafe*
Transport	*Bus 87 from Pitlochry or Blair Atholl*
Parking	*House of Bruar car park (free, PH18 5TW)*
Toilets	*House of Bruar*

Time 1hr
Distance 2.7km (1.7 miles)
Climb 130m

A classic loop of waterfalls and bridges on easy-to-follow paths first launched in the 18th-century

This walk starts on a comfortable well-maintained wide path to the fabulous stone bridge over the Lower Falls of Bruar before ascending on a narrower, possibly muddier, path to the Upper Falls, which are crossed on another fantastic stone bridge. It loops back gradually downhill on the other side of the Bruar stream, just in time for lunch or afternoon tea. Although there are no exposed sections along the path itself, it is important to stay on the path and heed the signs warning of steep edges above the gorge.

A walker checks the information board and map

SHORT WALKS PERTHSHIRE NORTH

On the lane by the House of Bruar shopping emporium and cafe

1 Leaving the car park, turn right onto the pavement along the main road and go first left between the House of Bruar and Bruar stream, following signs for the falls. Pass under the railway and soon, using the steps up onto the rocks, reach a first lookout towards the **Lower Falls**, the arched stone bridge and the wonderful natural black rock arch.

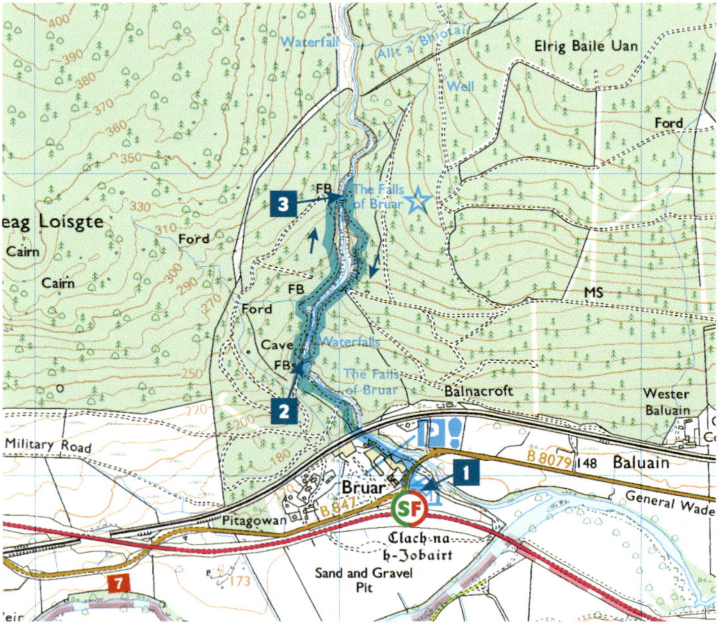

The rocks have been smoothed by the cascading waters

In the 18th century, the poet Robert Burns wrote 'The Humble Petition of Bruar Water' to the fourth Duke of Atholl requesting the creation of this path and surrounding reforestation.

The stone bridge over the Lower Falls blends in with the surrounding rocks

2 Return down the steps and turn right towards the bridge but continue ahead without crossing over the falls (which you shall do from the other side on the return). Admire the remains of one of the fanciful 18th-century viewpoints, then head onto a narrower path with rocks and roots underfoot. After some wooden steps, views emerge of the bridge from the other side. Having successfully completed all the uphill walking, reach the **Upper Falls** and another stone bridge.

3 Cross over the bridge and immediately turn right (there are benches in the trees on the left). Ignore all tracks from the left. Turn left over the Lower Falls bridge and retrace your steps back to the car park.

Views open up to hills that frame Glen Tilt

WALK 2
Glen Tilt and Blair Castle

Time 3hr
Distance 8.5km (5.3 miles)
Climb 230m

Start/finish	Glen Tilt car park, Blair Atholl
Locate	///bucks.afterglow.snuggled
Cafes/pubs	None on route
Transport	Train to Blair Atholl station 1.7km from start
Parking	Glen Tilt car park (free, PH18 5TX)
Toilets	No public toilets on route

Explore rolling countryside with views to the wilder moorland on higher hills and the sumptuous castle grounds of the Atholl Estate

Before entering the grounds of Blair Castle, this walk explores a combination of local trails: the green Farm and Forest Trail, the yellow Glen Tilt Trail and a detour onto the blue Balvenie Pillar Walk. With great views from country lanes and forest tracks, the route takes in Blair's soaring trees and surrounding high peaks. Note that the Castle grounds are closed from 1 November to 31 March, so during that time only the Glen Tilt loop can be completed, shortening the walk by 2km (1hr).

Blair Castle, the old seat of the Atholl dukes

SHORT WALKS PERTHSHIRE NORTH

1 From Glen Tilt car park (information board) head to the entrance road to the car park and turn left along it. Keep to the road at the fork, enjoying views towards hills and open countryside to reach the end of the road.

2 Turn right uphill along a country lane, soon passing a farmstead on the right followed by another on the left as more views unfold to Glen Tilt and the surrounding mountains. Ignore a left-hand track, keep right at the next fork, and shortly spot a path on the right leading downhill through woods, waymarked with a wooden post and little green arrow. This will be your route, but first continue ahead for 150m to pass through the gate of a shooting range for a wonderful viewpoint over Glen Tilt. This remote valley leads to the higher peaks of the Cairngorms National Park.

3 Retrace your steps to take the green-arrowed path, cross over a small waterfall on a wooden bridge and turn right onto a road that returns to Glen Tilt car park. After 1.3km, an optional right-hand detour (1km return), marked with a blue arrow, leads to the Balvenie Pillar.

> Set atop Tom Na Croiche (meaning 'hangman's knoll'), the rough rubble obelisk was erected in 1755 by the second Duke of Atholl on the site of the last public hanging on the estate in 1630.

A quick detour leads to one of Perthshire's fanciful 18th-century hermitages

4 Continue along the road. Several additional detours are possible before returning to the car park; they take you closer to the river and to a 1758 grotto, a curious example of one of Perthshire's unique hermitage structures. Built to entertain more adventurous guests, eccentric hermitages were constructed in the late 18th century, overlooking waterfalls and accentuating the wilderness. Just before entering Glen Tilt car park, turn right onto a wide track, known as the Hercules Walk (no vehicular access), that initially runs almost parallel to the now-familiar road. (In winter the walk finishes at this point as there is no access to the Castle grounds.)

Blair Castle's fairy-tale garden extends to approximately 2500 acres

WALK 2 – GLEN TILT AND BLAIR CASTLE

5 Very soon take the first gate into the walled Hercules Garden within the grounds of **Blair Castle**.

Dating back to the mid 18th century, the Hercules Garden contains a canal pond crossed by a Chinese bridge, an apple house, and the pavilion known as McGregor's Folly with an informative museum.

After exploring the garden however you choose, use the southwestern gate at the far end to turn right back onto the Hercules Walk, soon crossing a footbridge with Blair Castle ahead of you.

6 Facing the castle, turn right then follow information posts onto a path into woods on the right. Turn right onto the next path across Banvie Burn, go left at the fork and keep straight over all junctions to **St Bride's Kirk**.

The church is thought to date back to the late 16th century. Within the grounds, you can find heraldic treasures including a memorial to the sixth Duke of Atholl carved with a mourning Atholl Highlander.

7 Take the right-hand option by the church then turn right alongside the walls of the Hercules Garden (you can also keep ahead to reach the road by Glen Tilt car park). At the far end of the wall turn left back onto the Hercules Walk, this time passing the Hercules statue, and return to the car park. This 1743 life-size Hercules statue by John Cheere is one of the many imitations of the ancient Farnese Hercules.

Blair Castle

The grand seat of the Dukes of Atholl is one of Scotland's most prized castles. Set in romantic fairy-tale grounds, it is immensely popular with tourists and for weddings and other events. Atholl started as a Pictish kingdom and became an earldom in the early 12th century. Construction of the present building began in 1269 and the many alterations over subsequent centuries have given it its current asymmetry, topped with a baronial harling exterior from the 19th and 20th centuries. To this day, it is home to the only private army in Europe; the Atholl Highlanders escorted Queen Victoria upon her 1844 visit and thereafter were granted their rights to arms.

Rich woodland of mixed conifer plantations alongside native Scots pine and deciduous trees

WALK 3
South Loch Rannoch Forest Trail

Time 2hr 30min
Distance 8.3km (5.2 miles)
Climb 170m

A peaceful walk through ancient pine woodland with beautiful views over Loch Rannoch

Start/finish	*Loch Rannoch Forest car park by Carie, near Kinloch Rannoch*
Locate	*///outsmart.fills.euphoric*
Cafes/pubs	*None on route*
Transport	*No public transport*
Parking	*Loch Rannoch Forest car park (free, PH17 2QJ)*
Toilets	*Kilvrecht Campsite (500m from start, closed in winter)*

This waymarked walk travels above Allt na Bogair gorge on forest tracks, passing through ancient Scots pine of the native Caledonia Forest and mixed deciduous woodland with views to Loch Rannoch. The ground is uneven at times, there are a few slopes, and note that there is no phone signal in the area. On the forest floor, look out for delicious blaeberries (bilberries) between July and September.

About halfway, the walk skirts around a tranquil forest loch

WALK 3 – SOUTH LOCH RANNOCH FOREST TRAIL

1 From the car park (information board) go straight, passing a pretty footbridge on your left. The footbridge leads to Kilvrecht campsite and toilets (closed in winter). Promptly turn right onto a path, following a wooden post with a three-coloured top. Just after spotting the shelter and picnic tables on the right, turn right at a junction of paths. Head gently uphill and turn left at the T-junction along the wider track, now following the yellow-topped wooden posts.

2 Keeping ahead in the same direction, the track narrows and views to hills appear on the left as the sounds of the bubbling waters of **Allt na Bogair** crescendo below. After 2.8km, cross a little stream, then pass a waterfall, and descend to the burn by Scots pine trees. Look out for pine marten, red deer and red squirrels that are all particularly fond of seeds from these evergreen trees. By the burn, spot the bridge on the left, but instead turn right onto the path. Reach a track, turn right onto it and come to a tranquil forest lake.

> ⓘ *In the 18th century reforestation was instigated by the fourth Duke of Atholl, who planted an astonishing 27 million trees.*

Scotland's national tree, the Scots pine is the only native pine species in the UK

Views appear over Loch Rannoch with Kinloch Rannoch village in the distance

3 Head alongside the lake on the track but when it makes a left bend, keep straight on instead, taking the path ahead and following the yellow-topped post through the Black Wood.

Forestry and Land Scotland started to manage the Black Wood of Rannoch in 1947 and the woodland surrounding Loch Rannoch contains some of the largest areas of ancient pine forest in Scotland. This ancient woodland on the southern shore of the loch is now a Forest Nature Reserve and Site of Special Scientific Interest.

After about 700m turn right (no sign) onto a wide forestry road. Views towards Loch Rannoch appear. Pass a quarry on your right and, after 1km, head right onto an uphill path to a lovely viewpoint and bench. Loch Rannoch is Scotland's ninth largest freshwater lake. The name 'Rannoch' stems from the Scottish Gaelic word for 'fern' or 'bracken' and nearby Rannoch Moor is the biggest moor in Scotland.

4 Descend on the path behind the viewpoint. Turn left then right to retrace your steps to the car park.

WALK 4
Allean Forest Trail

Time 1hr 30min
Distance 4km (2.5 miles)
Climb 150m

Start/finish	Allean Forest car park
Locate	///punk.songbird.message
Cafes/pubs	None on route
Transport	82 bus from Pitlochry to Queen's View, then walk along the B8019 for 600m and turn right uphill for 100m to the start
Parking	Allean Forest car park (charge, PH16 5RH)
Toilets	Allean Forest car park

A wee ramble to two historic ruins: an 18th-century Clachan homestead and a Pictish fort

This pleasant short trail through forests, along grassy paths and firm gravel tracks, leads to the remains of an old Clachan settlement and Pictish hill fort homestead with views towards Loch Tummel and the mountains beyond. On your way to or back from the walk be sure to stop off at the magnificent Queen's View viewpoint, named to commemorate Queen Victoria's visit in 1866.

The remains of the Clachan community and the 'black house'

SHORT WALKS PERTHSHIRE NORTH

The walk follows the red Ring Fort Trail

1 From the car park, take the path uphill signed with yellow and red wooden posts and pass the toilets. Cross **Ardgualich Burn** on a wooden bridge, turn left along the forestry track, then turn left onto a path. Cross another burn, head downhill then up and soon reach the remains of a Clachan community (information board).

Clachans were 18th-century permanent self-sufficient settlements. At this specific site, the weathered yet well-preserved stones reveal the community's layout, and visitors can venture inside the 'black house', so-called owing to the stained walls caused by peat-fuelled fires.

Exploring inside the 'black house'

WALK 4 – ALLEAN FOREST TRAIL

2 After exploring, continue on the waymarked path. A very quick 20m signed detour on the left heads to a viewpoint, although mostly obscured by trees. Continue uphill more steeply in zigzags, cross a burn and go over a wide forest track to keep uphill on the path ahead. Turn right onto the next wide track and follow it to a junction.

3 Ignoring the yellow route departing on the right, continue to follow the red route. After 5min turn off onto a delightful downhill grassy path and, at the bottom, turn right onto a track following the wooden post just to the right. Reach the Iron Age Family Circle (information board) with views towards Loch Tummel and the cone-shaped mountain Schiehallion.

> The name Schiehallion means 'fairy mountain' and alludes to the mist that persistently envelops it. At 1083m high Schiehallion is a Munro, one of the Scottish mountains over 3000ft (914m). There are 282 Munros in total, of which Perthshire boasts 28.

4 Back on the track, the yellow trail joins back in. Shortly after, turn left onto the path back to the car park.

The last part of the walk offers views of Loch Tummel and Schiehallion

Northern Perthshire's early history

Prehistoric and early historical remains are scattered throughout Perthshire. Excavations commencing in the 1970s show that, having escaped the impacts of agriculture, upland Perthshire

The circular remains of an Iron Age family home

has preserved monuments dating as far back as the Neolithic period (4000–2000BC). These include stone circles, long cairns, chambered tombs and standing stones, mainly used for ceremonial rites. However, it is likely that the first settlers arrived via the Firth of Tay as early as 7000BC, during the post-glacial Mesolithic colonization. On this walk the Iron Age homestead, dating from 500BC–AD300, was then reused by the Picts in AD300–900.

WALK 5
Loch Faskally and Pitlochry salmon ladder

Time 2hr
Distance 5.2km (3.2 miles)
Climb 100m

A gentle walk on paths and roads explores Pitlochry's highlights dotted around Loch Faskally

Start/finish	Fisher's Hotel on Pitlochry's high street
Locate	///yacht.agrees.sofa
Cafes/pubs	Plenty in town, cafes at Pitlochry Boating Station and Adventure Hire (Fridays and weekends) and Pitlochry Dam Visitor Centre
Transport	Train to Pitlochry station. Bus 27 from Perth
Parking	SSE Pitlochry Dam car park (free, PH16 5AP), other car parks (charge) at Atholl Rd, train station, Rie-Achan Road and Ferry Rd
Toilets	On West Lane by Rie-Achan Road car park, near Pitlochry train station

This well-signed circuit highlights Pitlochry's characterful landmarks: the suspension bridge, the popular Festival Theatre, the impressive salmon fish ladder and hydroelectric dam (www.pitlochrydam.com), and Loch Faskally, all set amidst woodland which is especially lovely in autumn, with a marvellous array of colours. The route is completed on roads, paths and steps.

Clear signs provide distances in miles to key locations

SHORT WALKS PERTHSHIRE NORTH

1 With your back to the hotel, turn right down the high street. Pass the War Memorial cross and immediately turn right, following black and golden signs for the Festival Theatre, the fish ladder and the dam. Go under the railway and pass Ferry Road car park. Keeping the restaurant on your right, continue along Ferry Road then take a left-hand path (signs) to reach the **Port na Craig** green suspension bridge over the River Tummel.

Long before the iron bridge was constructed in 1913, 12th-century monks used a ferry boat chained to the rock in the centre of the river to secure against dangerous currents. Craig comes from the Gaelic '*creag*' meaning 'rock'.

2 Once across the bridge, turn right along the road (signs). Pass the glass-fronted Pitlochry Festival Theatre. Upon reaching the bottom of

Walkers stop to enjoy the colours on a grey day

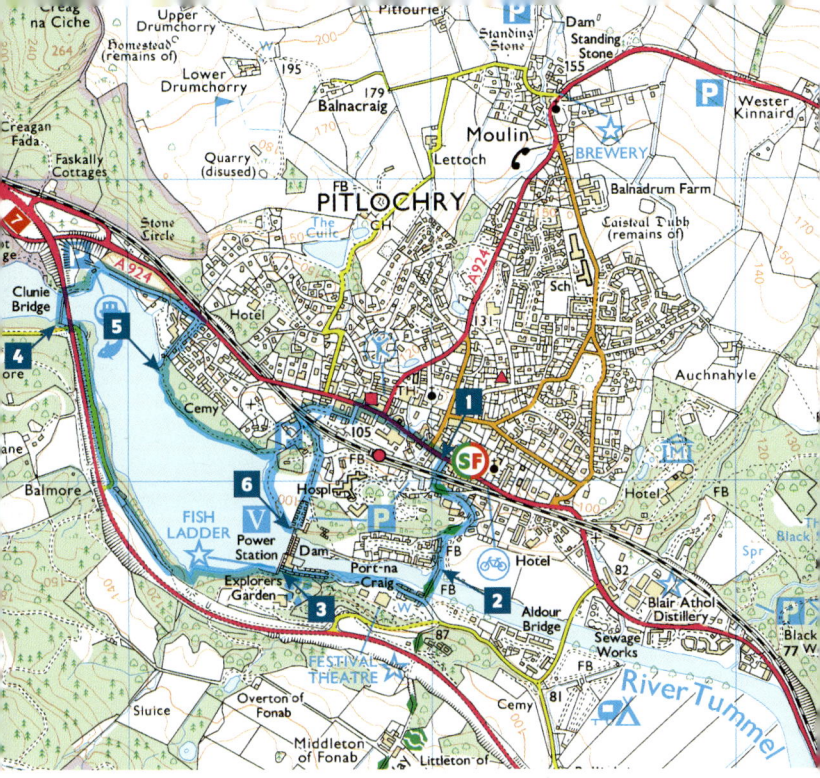

the **salmon ladder**, take a left-hand path uphill, then a series of steps on the left by the dam, and start a loop around **Loch Faskally**.

> The salmon ladder was constructed alongside the hydroelectric dam in the mid 20th century. One of the 34 tiered pools has a chamber where you can spot some of the 5000 salmon that annually swim upstream back to their spawning grounds.

3 The path goes down steps, over a little bridge, up steeper steps and touches down on a minor road by a house almost adjacent to the A9. Turn right and follow the minor road under the A9, then immediately take the right-hand path (signed for the boating station).

4 Turn right onto the **Clunie footbridge** across the river, pass the boating station and cafe, turn right onto an uphill lane and, before it veers left,

SHORT WALKS PERTHSHIRE NORTH

take Lagreach Brae road on the right (signed for the dam). Where the road bends left take the signed right-hand path to the shores of the loch.

5 From this point, stay on the paths closest to the water to reach the dam and visitor centre. Pitlochry's massive concrete dam – Perthshire's biggest civil engineering project – was constructed between 1947 and 1951.

6 After your explorations, leave on the road. Pass the dam car park, head under the railway, and, at the end of the road, turn left back to the high street and then turn right to return to your start point.

— To shorten

At Waypoint 3 go across the dam, skipping the Loch Faskally section of the walk (2.3km, 45min), or only complete the Loch Faskally portion using the dam and Clunie bridge (4.2km, 1hr 30min).

From the dam there are fantastic views back to the suspension bridge and Perthshire's green countryside

The footbridge and A9 cross Loch Faskally

Pitlochry

Pitlochry grew in 1728 when General Wade's new military road was constructed to link Dunkeld and Inverness. An important stopover, the town thrived throughout the 19th century; it replaced Birnam as the Highland Railway's terminus and transformed into a popular resort town. Mills, distilleries and the town's stone buildings all date from that period. The colossal French-style Atholl Palace Hotel was built as a hydropathic spa when the therapy became fashionable in 19th-century Perthshire. The town remains a favoured destination where a picturesque, lively high street with gabled buildings is enveloped in outstanding scenery.

The salmon ladder and hydroelectric dam have become representative of Pitlochry

Cairn and trig point on the top of Ben Vrackie

WALK 6
Ben Vrackie

Time 4hr 30min
Distance 8.6km (5.3 miles)
Climb 645m

A local favourite, Ben Vrackie offers the same breath-taking summit experience as any of Scotland's highest peaks

Start/finish	*Ben Vrackie car park*
Locate	*///persuade.exploring.orchestra*
Cafes/pubs	*None on route*
Transport	*No public transport*
Parking	*Ben Vrackie car park (free, PH16 5EL), overflow car park located 290m away down the road before the main one*
Toilets	*No public toilets on route*

Ben Vrackie (meaning 'speckled mountain') is an 814m-tall Corbett (a mountain between 2500ft and 3000ft) that watches proudly over Pitlochry. On a clear day, the summit beckons enticingly, and it's no wonder that it is northern Perthshire's most trodden mountain, owing to good signage, heather-blanketed slopes and breath-taking views. It is not to be underestimated; the steep climb gets the heart pumping, and the descent requires attentiveness and sturdy footwear.

The last green sign points the way up Ben Vrackie

SHORT WALKS PERTHSHIRE NORTH

Benches with beautiful views offer a place to take a rest along the walk

1 At the main car park turn left through the tunnel of trees along a wide path, with **Moulin Burn** on your right-hand side. Head up wooden steps, pass through a gate, go up more steps and over the burn. Cross over the track, pass through a deer fence gate then by a bench, and turn left to join a gravel track. Promptly leave the track onto a narrow gravel path ahead that goes over two burns to reach another gate in the deer fence.

2 Pass through the gate and tread carefully over stepping stones into open moorland as the stone-strewn summit of Ben Vrackie appears. The obvious path starts to reveal views back to Pitlochry, with two conveniently positioned benches along the way. Further, a green sign points the way at a crossroads. This is the final green sign, but soon a little purple arrow emerges on a swing gate. At the next fork keep left on the path towards the left-hand big knoll called **Stac an Fheidh**.

3 A little further, cross a track, then head downhill to skirt around Stac an Fheidh, arriving at the shimmering **Loch a'Choire** mountain lake. Keeping it on your left reach a bench.

> ⓘ *Perthshire is nicknamed 'gateway to the Highlands'; what stretches beyond this frontier are the steeper, more rugged and wilder territories of Scotland's Highlands, both in terms of terrain and legends.*

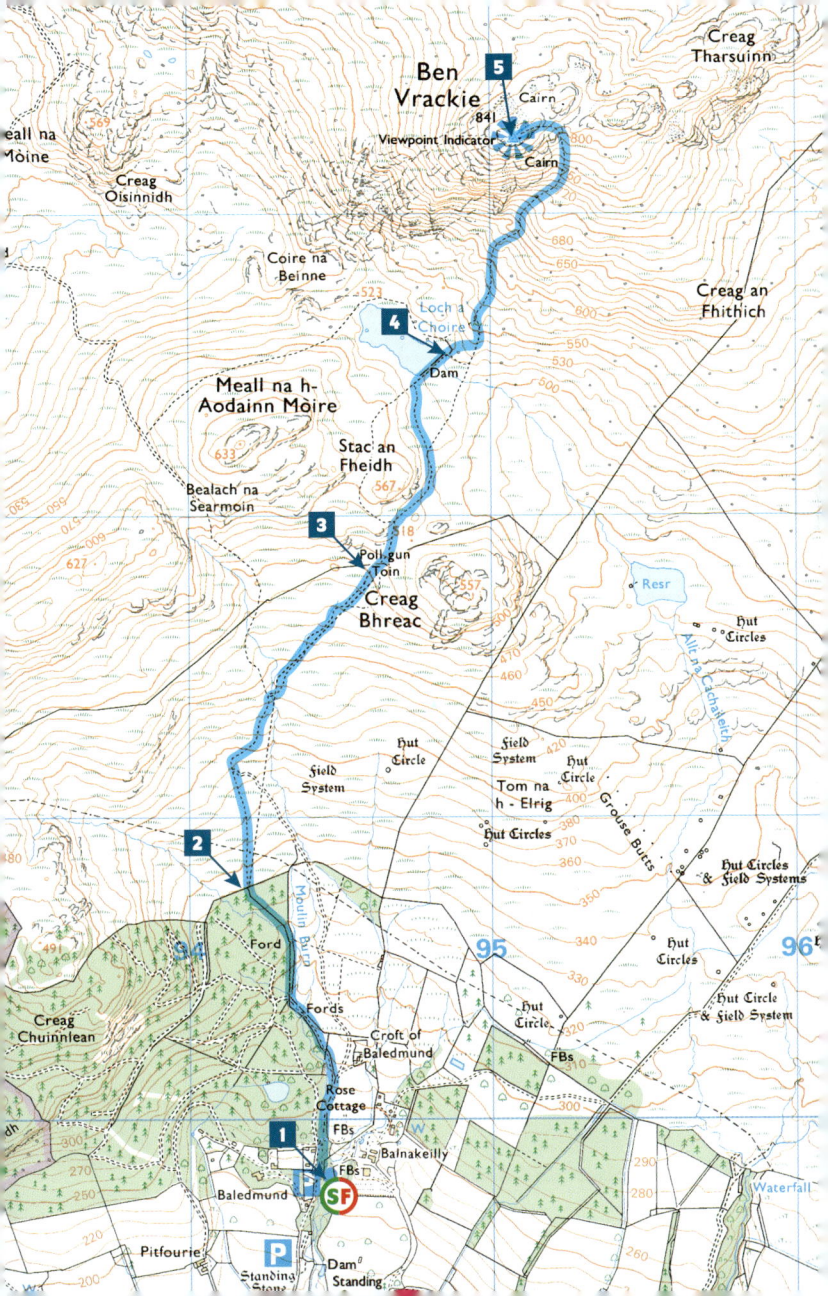

The sun begins to set behind Loch a Choire

The final ascent on stone steps and paths, surrounded by heather-clad slopes

4 Use the stepping stones to pass over **Alt na Cachaileith** burn and climb steps to begin the steep ascent up to the summit. Always keeping to the evident path, reach the top of **Ben Vrackie** with its cairn, trig point and orientation table.

Give yourself a well-deserved rest amidst exquisite 360-degree panoramas: Pitlochry and its southern forested hills, the eastern Blair Atholl Munros, the northerly mountains of the Cairngorms National Park, and the flatter eastern landscapes of Angus that sweep towards the North Sea.

5 From the summit, return the same way to the start.

The classification of Scotland's summits

Views towards the Blair Atholl Munros from the summit of Ben Vrackie

Scotland's hilltops and mountain peaks are grouped into four major categories, named after those who created the listings that are still adhered to today. The 282 Munros have a minimum elevation of 3000ft (914m). They are followed by 222 Corbetts that reach heights between 2500ft (762m) and 3000ft. The 244 Grahams have summits between 2000ft (610m) and 2500ft, and they must also have a minimum prominence drop of 492ft (150m); these are the same requirements to be classed as a 'mountain' in the UK. Finally, the 89 Donalds exceed 2000ft but do not meet the prominence drop criteria.

Crossing the sheep field where the overgrown ruins of the Black Castle lie

WALK 7
Black Spout and two distilleries

Start/finish	Fisher's Hotel on Pitlochry's high street
Locate	///yacht.agrees.sofa
Cafes/pubs	Plenty in town, hotel/pub in Moulin, bar at Blair Athol Distillery
Transport	Train to Pitlochry station. Bus 27 from Perth
Parking	Atholl Rd car park (charge, PH16 5BX), other car parks (charge) at train station, Rie-Achan Road and Ferry Rd
Toilets	On West Lane by Rie-Achan Road car park, near Pitlochry train station

Time 2hr
Distance 6.5km (4 miles)
Climb 130m

Moulin Church and village hall, castle ruins, meadows, woods and a waterfall are rounded off with two distilleries

This peaceful walk on good paths delights in its variety: the quaint village of Moulin, 13th-century castle ruins, views towards Pitlochry's soaring Ben Vrackie mountain, oak woods, the mighty Black Spout waterfall and two traditional whisky distilleries. Follow walking directions carefully to complete the full trail – signs on the ground can mislead towards alternatives and shortcuts.

Blair Athol distillery

SHORT WALKS PERTHSHIRE NORTH

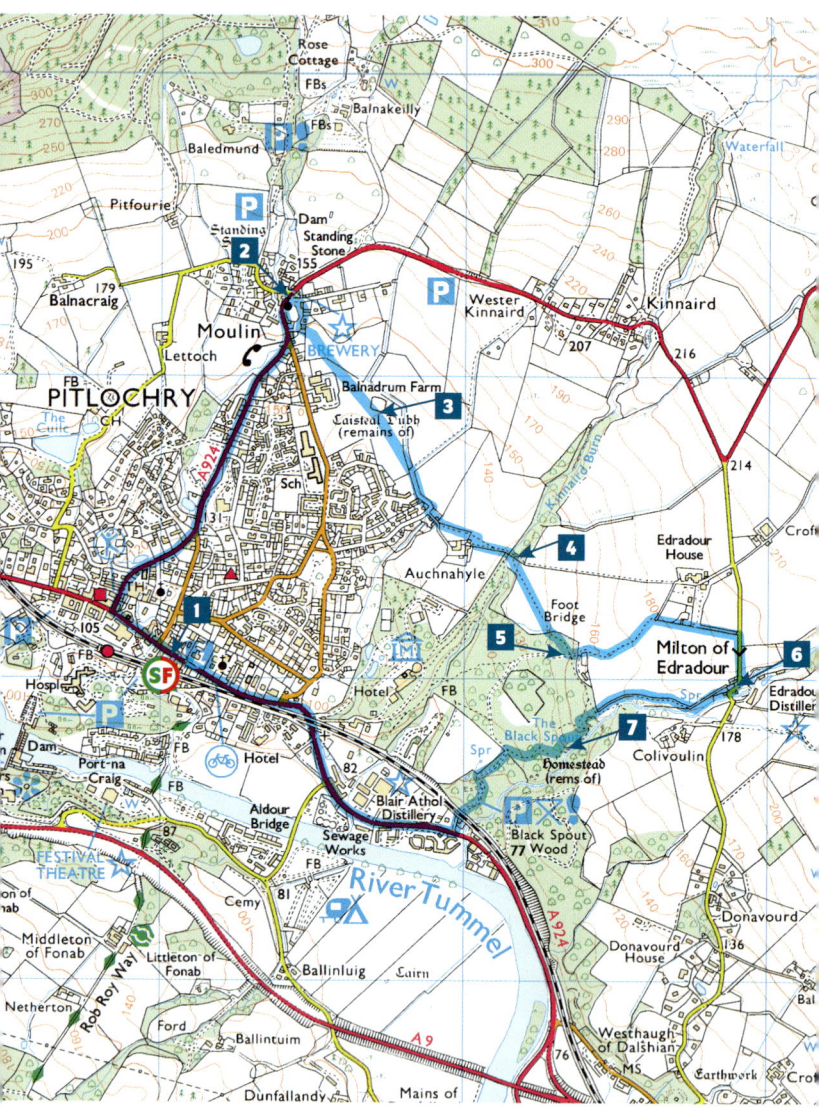

44

WALK 7 – BLACK SPOUT AND TWO DISTILLERIES

1 Turn left along the high street, cross it and go right, up West Moulin Road, reaching the village of **Moulin** with its hotel and church after about 15min. Moulin Church (1830–1831) was constructed on the site of a pre-Reformation church. The tower was rebuilt after a fire in 1873.

2 Turn right around the church grounds and, at the fork, keep right to Moulin Village Hall after which veer left to take the kissing gate (information board) into the field. Pass under electric lines and by a walking sign as you approach the humble ruins of **Caisteal Dubh Mhasthlinne**. These ailing fragments are all that remain of Moulin's 13th-century Black Castle that was set on fire to combat the plague in the early 16th century.

3 From the ruins, continue to the far end of the field. Take a gate into woods, following a path beside a stream, then keep the fence of a house on your right. Back on a road, veer left twice, then take a path by a blurred sign that runs parallel to another field and a road, spotting towering Ben Vrackie in the distance on your left. Head down steps, through a gate, and follow the sign to Edradour over a stream into the lovely **Black Spout Woods**.

4 After keeping right at the fork, cut directly across a wheat field, although after rainfall your shoes and socks may

Built in 1851, Moulin Village Hall was used as a school for a century

stay cleaner if you skirt around the field instead. On the other side of the field, go through a kissing gate, over a bridge, up some steps, and continue following signs for Edradour, rather than the Black Spout waterfall (unless you choose to shorten the walk), to reach a crossroads.

5 At the crossroads, take the left-hand track, then turn right onto a path to go right again alongside the grounds of pristine **Edradour House** and its driveway, at the end of which turn right onto a downhill road. Soon the distinguishable white buildings of the **Edradour Distillery** with their red timber framing appear past the stone bridge ahead. Charming Edradour is Scotland's smallest distillery and retains most of its original 1825 features.

6 To continue, just before the bridge, turn right onto a gravel path alongside a house, following the sign for Pitlochry. This section weaves its way through woods above **Edradour Burn**. After a stretch by a pretty moss-covered drystone wall and then a sign for the Black Spout, ignore a right-hand path to keep ahead downhill, reaching a section that can be a little overgrown. For this next part, look out for white arrows drawn into a yellow circle. All little paths along here lead down to a left turn towards a makeshift shelter made of twigs. Here, turn left following signs for the waterfall, and listen to the burn gaining momentum. A wooden

In dry weather you can cut directly across the wheat field

Black Spout waterfall cascades through the summer foliage

railing appears to prevent erosion on the banks of the gorge, before the viewing platform is reached on the left and the many layers of the 60m **Black Spout falls** are unveiled.

7 Back on the path, keep to the yellow arrows on green circular backgrounds downhill into woods (instead of following the wooden railing). At a crossroads, follow the painted pointing yellow figure, turn left onto a wide semi-paved track, pass a golf course then the car park for the falls on the left. Go under the railway, turn right along the main road into town and pass **Blair Athol Distillery** and Holy Trinity Episcopal Church. Blair Athol Distillery, popular for its tours and tastings, is one of Scotland's oldest distilleries, established in 1789. Immediately cross over the main road onto Bruach Lane to use the

Heading back to town, the route goes downhill through woods

pedestrian walkway under the railway. Pass the entrance to Atholl Palace Hotel and find yourself back on the high street.

> **− To shorten**
>
> To save 1.4km (20min) at Waypoint 5, follow signs directly to the waterfall, skipping Edradour Distillery, and rejoin the main route from Waypoint 7.

Restaurants and beer gardens on the banks of the Tay in Dunkeld

WALK 8
Inver Path and Pine Cone Point

Time 3hr
Distance 10.8km (6.7 miles)
Climb 260m

A forested uphill hike leads to a lovely viewpoint before meanderings along the Tay reveal Dunkeld's cathedral and famous bridge

Start/finish	The Hermitage car park near Dunkeld
Locate	///alley.misted.mountain
Cafes/pubs	Mobile cafe in car park (closed Mon and Tue)
Transport	No public transport to start. Dunkeld is a 2km walk away (see Walk 9 for walking directions and Walk 10 for transport to Dunkeld)
Parking	The Hermitage car park (charge, PH8 0JR)
Toilets	The Hermitage car park

Dunkeld has a fantastic network of signed walking trails. This popular walk combines the Inver Path with an invigorating although gradual trek up on tracks to Pine Cone Point, which overlooks Dunkeld's harmonious valley and hills. The last section is downhill and then flat, following the serpentine River Tay to views of the town's wonderful cathedral and bridge.

The rather eccentric Torryvald viewpoint makes for a good snack break

SHORT WALKS PERTHSHIRE NORTH

1 From the car park (information board) follow signs for the Hermitage to the left of the toilets, keeping the **Braan river** on your left. The path widens into a track. This is part of an old military road. At the fork, keep to the track rather than the path (ignoring the waymarks with the black crown image) to reach the next crossroads of tracks.

2 At the crossroads go right, then keep ahead at the next junction to follow signs onto a left-hand uphill track to Pine Cone Point. Turn right onto

the next track and right again, still uphill, to the pine cone-shaped viewpoint. Take a well-earned rest here to look out north towards the forested slopes that frame the Tay river.

Pine Cone viewpoint lives up to its name

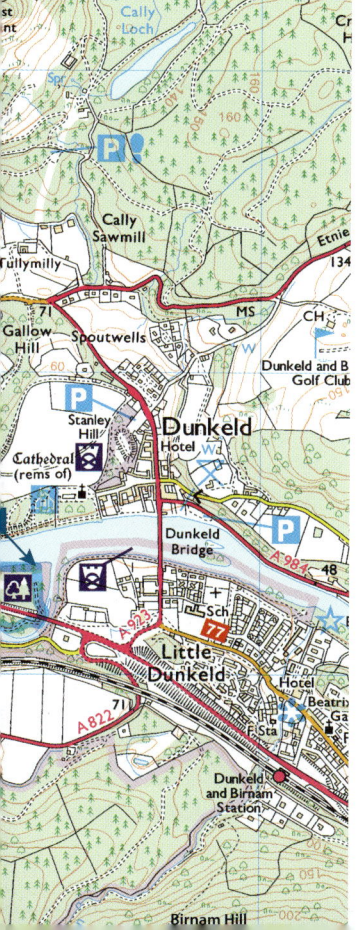

3 Descend the same way down to the signs and back to the track crossroads.

4 This time turn left along the track and promptly reach the peculiar, rocky Victorian Torryvald viewpoint a little way to your right, an opportunity to rest after having covered almost half the distance and all the uphill walking. Back on route, go right at the next junction and immediately left onto a very steep downhill grassy path through the Douglas Fir Woods. Turn right at the bottom to reach the **forestry car park**.

The Douglas Fir Woods are named after a proud north American conifer that once stood by the famous Ossian's Hall (see Walk 9). At 63m high, it was one of Britain's highest trees before strong winds blew it over in 2017.

5 Cross the car park then the road and take the path directly ahead into woods. Cross over a lane and pass

The River Tay and Dunkeld Bridge

under the railway and the A9 to start a lovely walk beside the **River Tay**. Cross two streams, then, at a fork, keep left nearest the river as views of Dunkeld Cathedral and the town's bridge appear across the waters.

> ⓘ *The Tay, Scotland's longest river, was hailed by the early Roman legionary troops as a second Tiber.*

Dunkeld's fine cathedral was built around its choir in the mid 13th century. Originally, this location was a site of pilgrimage for followers of St Columba after Kenneth MacAplin, first king of both the Picts and the Scots, brought the saint's relics here in 849.

6 Find yourself inevitably turning right, away from the Tay, to head under the **A9** and alongside the Braan river, and soon reach a fork.

7 Be sure to fork right onto a track (rather than taking the road), entering the village of **Inver**. Turn right onto the road past houses, and, at the end of the road, use a path by the A9 to reach a left turn onto the access road to the Hermitage car park.

− To shorten
From Pine Cone Point walk back the same way you came, totalling 5.3km (2hr 30min) return.

+ To lengthen
Combine this route with Walk 9.

Dunkeld

Dunkeld is a splendid small town and attracts visitors enthralled by its heritage as well as keen mountain bikers seeking adrenaline on the local craggy slopes. From the Middle Ages, it was one of Scotland's most important ecclesiastical centres. Following their victory at the 1689 Battle of Killicrankie, Jacobite forces burned down most of the town's houses in the Battle of Dunkeld, yet a year later, pretty homes were rebuilt on Cathedral Street, visible today thanks to the National Trust for Scotland's 'Little Houses' restoration scheme during the 1950s. At the heart of the old marketplace, known as The Cross, the 1866 fountain in Gothic style commemorates the sixth Duke of Atholl. The name Dunkeld is translated from the Gaelic *Dùn Chaillean* as 'Fort of the Caledonians', referring to a local Pictish tribal group.

Gothic-style fountain in the old marketplace in Dunkeld

The tumultuous falls on the River Braan

WALK 9
The Braan and Inchewan paths

Start/finish	The Hermitage car park near Dunkeld
Locate	///alley.misted.mountain
Cafes/pubs	Mobile cafe in car park (closed Mon and Tue)
Transport	No public transport. Dunkeld is a 2km walk away (see Walk 9 for walking directions and Walk 10 for transport to Dunkeld)
Parking	The Hermitage car park (charge, PH8 0JR)
Toilets	The Hermitage car park

Time 3hr
Distance 10.2km (6.3 miles)
Climb 250m

One of the most visited sites in northern Perthshire, the dramatic Hermitage is a whimsical highlight of any trip

One of Perthshire's undeniable classics, this walk on comfortable paths and tracks meanders through woodland beside the Braan and Inchewan rivers, and through gentle rolling fields. The highlights of the walk are the celebrated Hermitage – composed of Ossian's Hall, a precipitous folly, and a rustic stone arch over the gorge – and the sensational Rumbling Bridge over the roaring Braan Falls.

Ossian's Hall was first built in 1757 with mirrors bringing to life the waterfalls from within

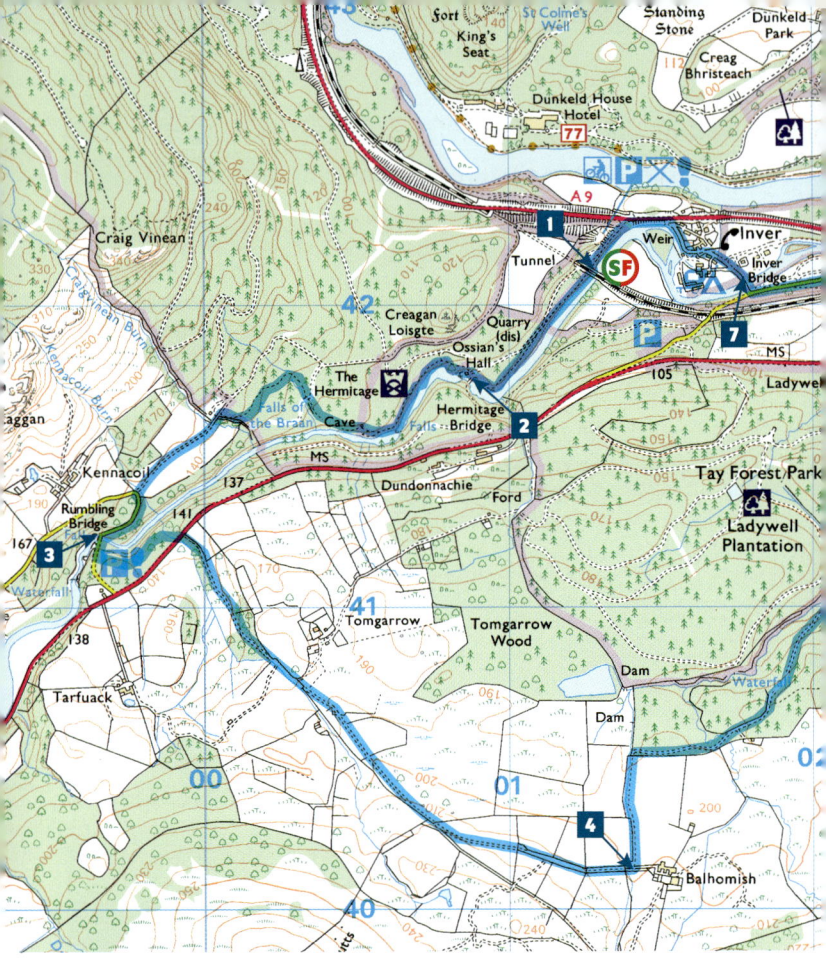

> ⓘ In the 18th century, landowners built thrilling hermitages and viewing platforms to dramatise the beauty of wild waterfalls, to the delight of their wilderness-seeking guests.

1 From the car park (information board) follow waymarks for the Hermitage, keeping the **River Braan** on your left. The path widens into a track and, at the fork, ensure you take the path closest to the river, following waymarks with the black crown

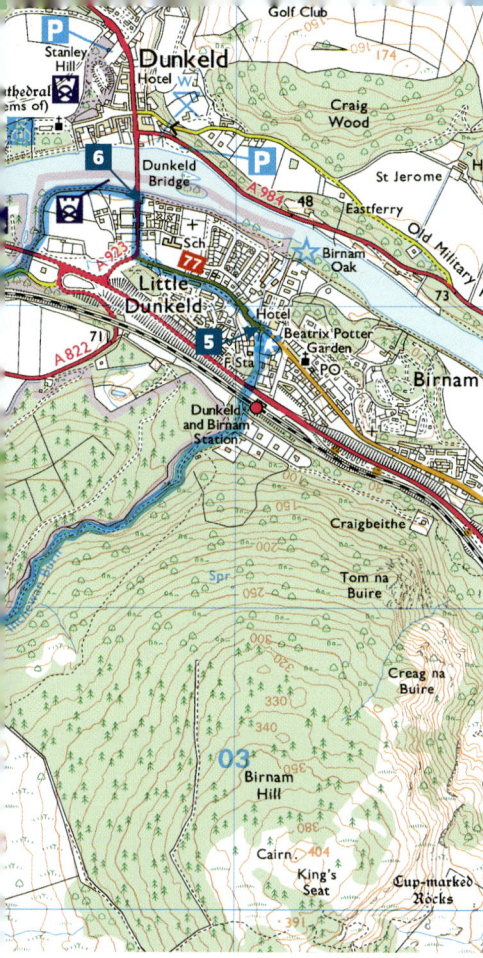

at first glance, but through its curtained entrance a hall of mirrors reflected the resplendence of the trio of cascades. The restored building of 1951 still impresses visitors and is a popular setting for weddings.

2 Continue on the same path, looking back to Ossian's Hall, keeping close to the **Braan Falls**. Pass the man-made cave, ignore first a right-hand then left-hand track. At the T-junction, turn left over a stream then go through a gate onto a fern-lined path that opens up to views of forested hills. Turn left onto the road and cross over the Braan Falls on **Rumbling Bridge**, which lives up to its name as the torrents crash below.

3 Almost immediately follow signs for the Braan Path left onto a narrow dirt path

symbol. Repeatedly keep to the riverside paths to reach **Ossian's Hall** and the stone bridge.

> Overlooking the impressive Braan Falls, the original 1757 Ossian's Hall was akin to a summerhouse

into woods and pass viewpoints to the falls. Upon reaching the A822, cross over with care onto the farm lane ahead. Ignoring all left-hand options, and with distant vistas to Craig Obney hill ahead and Birnam Hill to the left, reach **Balhomish** farmstead.

The precipitous folly of Ossian's Hall and rustic stone arch over the gorge

4 Turn left then keep to the track as it turns sharp right. Leave it at the next fork by bearing left. Surrounded by heather, keep downhill then turn right at the next T-junction onto a wider track entering Birnam Woods accompanied by **Inchewan Burn**. After 15min go through the gate with stone

The River Braan gains momentum to fall dramatically under Rumbling Bridge

WALK 9 – THE BRAAN AND INCHEWAN PATHS

The walk follows Dunkeld's popular Braan and Inchewan paths

pillars, then bear right and left onto a narrow gravel path under the railway to avoid the vehicular tunnel. Pass under the A9 and arrive in **Birnam** with the **Beatrix Potter Garden** along the road on the right.

5 At the end of the road turn left onto Perth Road. Promptly find a pedestrian walkway and cycle path on the left and briefly walk through a park before returning to Perth Road and through **Little Dunkeld**. At the end of the road turn right towards Dunkeld.

6 When you arrive at the start of **Dunkeld Bridge**, do not cross over but, on the right-hand side of the road, find a sign sending you down stone steps under the old toll-house building. Turn left under the bridge, following the Tay river, then pass under the A9. At the T-junction turn right onto the road, pass cream-coloured holiday lodges and enter the village of **Inver**.

7 Take the stone bridge over the River Braan and, at the end of the road, use a path by the A9 to reach a left turn onto the access road to the Hermitage car park.

> **− To shorten**
> Walk to the Hermitage and back (1.3km, 30min return).
>
> **+ To lengthen**
> Combine this route with Walk 8.

The trail makes its way through heather

WALK 10
Birnam Hill

Start/finish	*Dunkeld Cathedral*
Locate	*///awkward.plod.earl*
Cafes/pubs	*Plenty in Dunkeld and in Birnam*
Transport	*Train to Dunkeld & Birnam station. M91 bus from Edinburgh, Perth and Inverness, and local bus lines*
Parking	*North/Atholl Street car park (charge, PH8 0AR), other car parks at Tay Terrace (charge) and train station (free)*
Toilets	*North/Atholl Street car park*

Time 3hr 15min
Distance 8.5km (5.3 miles)
Climb 400m

After a steep intensive climb, a rewarding panorama stretches for miles at the King's Seat on top of Birnam Hill

After a potter through town, this walk quickly becomes one of the hardest in this guidebook due to a steep (though not exposed) climb up Birnam Hill through Birnam Wood. The splendid vistas stretch for miles and reward all the efforts made. It is well signed, but paths may be quite muddy and slippery so, after rainfall, sturdy footwear is advisable.

Dunkeld sits in a punchbowl surrounded by woodland and rugged hills

WALK 10 – BIRNAM HILL

Sculptures in the Beatrix Potter Garden in Birnam

1 With your back to the cathedral, leave the cathedral grounds through the elegant iron gates. Pass the traditional houses on Cathedral Street, the tourist information office and intricate central fountain, then turn right onto the high street and cross over the Tay river on picturesque **Dunkeld Bridge**.

> By the 18th century the last medieval bridge had fallen, and ferries replaced it until 1805, when Thomas Telford pioneered Dunkeld's fine mock-fortified 208m-long bridge, boasting five segmental arches and semi-circular turrets. One of the accompanying toll houses survives.

2 Continue along the road. Nearly out of town, turn left into the park. The fiddler statue commemorates Neil Gow, a local 18th-century musician

> ⓘ Beatrix Potter wrote both *The Tale of Peter Rabbit* **and** *The Tale of Jeremy Fisher* **in Aberfeldy.**

well known across Scotland. Turn left onto Perth Road, cross over, and promptly pick up the cycle/pedestrian path on the right into another park before returning onto Perth Road. On the corner with the **Beatrix Potter Garden** turn right, pass under the A9, then take the path that goes to the left of the railway bridge (avoiding the vehicular tunnel).

> As a child, Beatrix Potter spent many summers in Perthshire with her father, and her stays inspired some of her most-loved stories. The garden was laid out between 1991 and 1992 with charming bronze sculptures of her animal protagonists.

The King's Seat is the highest point on this walk at 393m

3 Cross the road and take the track directly ahead into Birnam Wood, soon reaching signs for a left turn up **Birnam Hill** by a tiny bench on a tree. Turn left onto the hill path and keep to the wider paths to avoid shortcuts that are often steeper. After making a few zigzag turns, emerge into a clearing, fork right, and keep uphill back into woods, always taking the more obviously trodden path. The path becomes a little rougher, with more tree roots and stones, as views begin to emerge on the left. It then steepens and reaches rocks that form the first viewpoint. Scramble up the rocks or go around to enjoy the vistas. Return to the path, which flattens and narrows as it heads through heather, before a steeper section to the **King's Seat** summit with its circular stone shelter.

Like many of the hilltop forts in Perthshire, it is likely that the King's Seat was used from 1000BC through to the Pictish period (AD1–500), including by the Romans.

4 Descend from the summit and follow the sign for the quarry, turn left or go straight down the rocks, and turn left onto a wider path taking you down wooden steps. Keep left again on the more obvious path to avoid a steep muddy descent. At a junction with a metal bench on the right, turn left towards the valley floor. The path passes through meadows of ferns and heather before re-entering Birnam Wood. Pass the first ruins and slates of the former quarry before reaching **Birnam Quarry** itself.

WALK 10 – BIRNAM HILL

5 At the quarry, take the forest road, then turn left onto a narrow path, ignoring a white arrow on a circular red background. The path widens into a track then becomes a road, arriving at the right-hand turn by the railway bridge passed earlier.

6 From here, turn right and retrace your steps back to **Dunkeld**.

Peacock butterfly (Aglais io) on buddleia along the forest road

– To shorten
Climb King's Seat and return to Dunkeld the same way, giving a walk of 6.9km (2hr 30min) return. Alternatively, start at Dunkeld and Birnam train station, saving 3km overall (50min).

+ To lengthen
Combine this route with Walk 9.

Birnam Wood

Birnam Wood is famous from the prophecy of Shakespeare's witches in his play *Macbeth*. The three Weird Sisters predict that Macbeth will be king of Scotland until Birnam Wood comes to Dunsinane. Because trees can't move, Macbeth believes this to be impossible, but the prophecy comes true when the English army uses branches of trees from Birnam Wood to camouflage its advance. Shakespeare visited Perth and Birnam in 1599 as part of a comedy troupe requested by King James VI. Two survivors of the old great forest, the Birnam Oak and the Birnam Sycamore, can be found on the south bank of the Tay in Birnam, and are listed among the 100 Scottish Heritage Trees. Perthshire itself boasts more Champion Trees than anywhere else in the UK and is nicknamed 'Big Tree Country'.

The track follows the disused railway

WALK 11
From Aberfeldy to Grandtully along the Tay

Time 2hr 30min
Distance 8km (5 miles)
Climb 65m

A section of the famous Rob Roy Way along the Tay and a disused railway take you from a splendid town to a pretty village

Start	The Birks Cinema, Aberfeldy
Finish	Grandtully Hotel, Grandtully
Locate	///poetic.should.fizzy
Cafes/pubs	In Aberfeldy and Grandtully
Transport	Bus 24 from Pitlochry changing at stop 'Inn' in Ballinluig for bus 23 or 23X from Dunkeld, several buses from Perth. From Grandtully buses run to Aberfeldy every 1hr 30min
Parking	Residential side streets off high street, car parks at Birks of Aberfeldy (free, PH15 2LD) and Moness Terrace (free, PH15 2AF)
Toilets	The Birks Cinema

Straightforward river paths alongside meadows framed by birch trees and a wide track through woodland along the disused railway connect Aberfeldy to the charming village of Grandtully (pronounced 'Grantly'). The calm waters of the Tay escalate to exhilarating rapids popular with keen canoeists and rafters. This trail is part of the last stretch on the multi-day Rob Roy Way and can be prolonged all the way to Pitlochry.

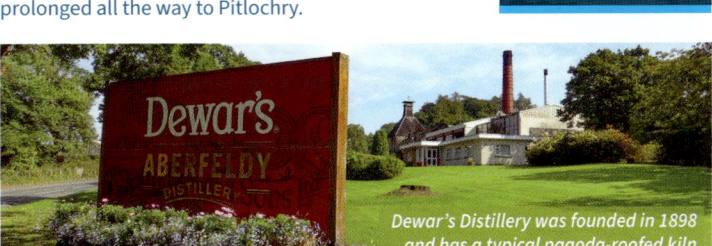

Dewar's Distillery was founded in 1898 and has a typical pagoda-roofed kiln

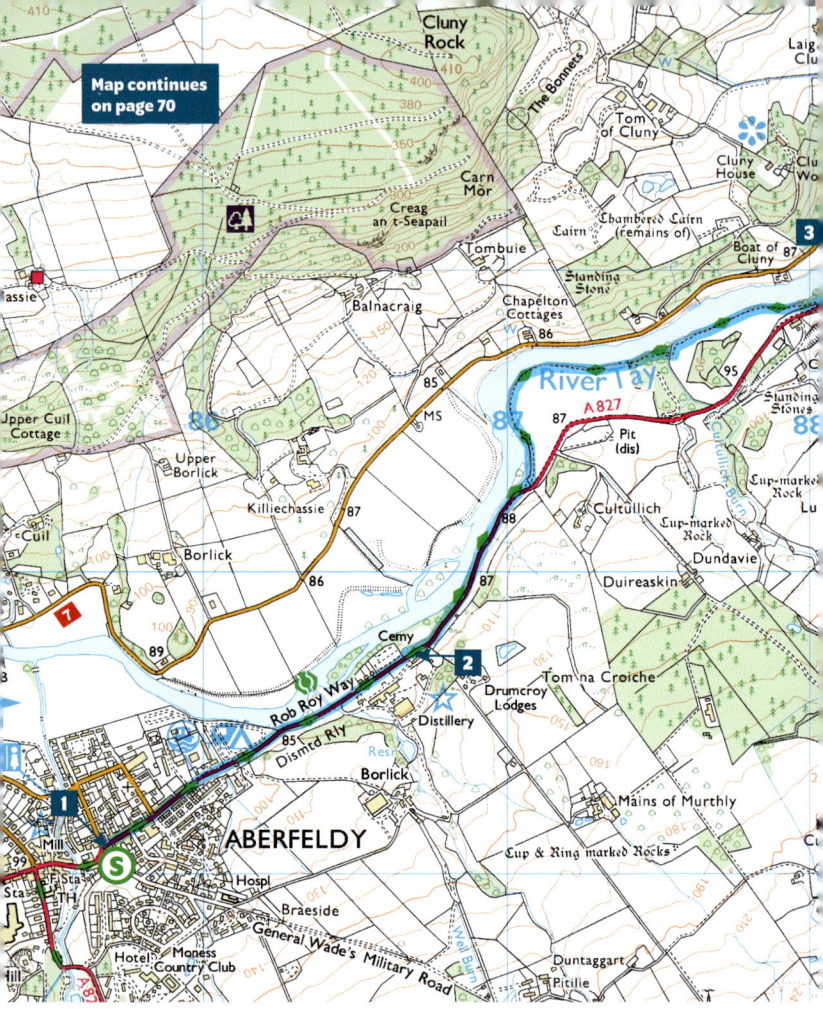

1 With your back to the cinema in **Aberfeldy**, turn left along the high street, also the A827, pass the caravan park, then pass the old railway bridge just up the lane on the right, a bench, Dewar's distillery and the cemetery on the left. Dewar's Distillery was founded in 1898. At its centre is the traditional pagoda-like ventilator of the kiln building.

WALK 11 – FROM ABERFELDY TO GRANDTULLY ALONG THE TAY

2 Alongside the watersports adventure centre on the left turn onto the signed path that at first runs along the inside of the fence parallel to the A827. Zigzag downhill to the **River Tay**. Go through a gate, over a burn, through another gate, and eventually head up to the wider track that follows the disused railway.

> The Aberfeldy–Ballinluig branch railway opened in 1865. It crossed 41 bridges, making it more expensive to build than any other line of the 249 miles of the Highland Railway Company. Closing barely 100 years later, some sections have now been repurposed for walkers and cyclists.

3 Continue to follow the **Rob Roy Way** along the dismantled railway. After 30min or so, ignore a left-hand path down to the river, and keep to the main track to reach a fork after a further 15min.

4 Here you have two options: you can either keep to the track or, as recommended, head back down to the Tay on the dirt track. By the river, pass a wooden hut with a bench and a stone jetty with lovely river views. Shortly after, cross a wooden bridge and skirt around fields. Cross a stream and head uphill to turn left back onto the disused railway.

5 Some 260m later, turn right and then left along the A827's grassy verge.

Maples flourish thanks to rainy days

The Tay was a key communication route for trade, industry, sustenance and fishing

> ⓘ *Many area, town and village names in Perthshire incorporate the word 'strath', which refers to their location in wide valleys.*

At the traffic lights, cross the main road carefully onto a right-hand lane (thus avoiding a dangerous bend on the A827). Veer left with the lane, following signs for the village centre, and pass Grandtully station campsite, which is located at the site of the old railway station. Reach the A827, now in **Grandtully**, and turn right for services and the Grandtully Hotel. Opposite the chocolate shop a left-hand road leads to the fabulous green iron bridge over the Tay.

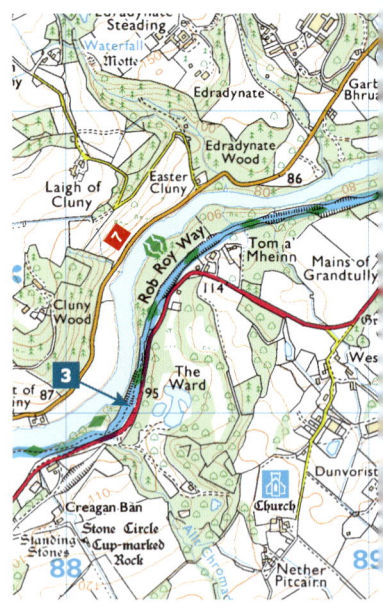

WALK 11 – FROM ABERFELDY TO GRANDTULLY ALONG THE TAY

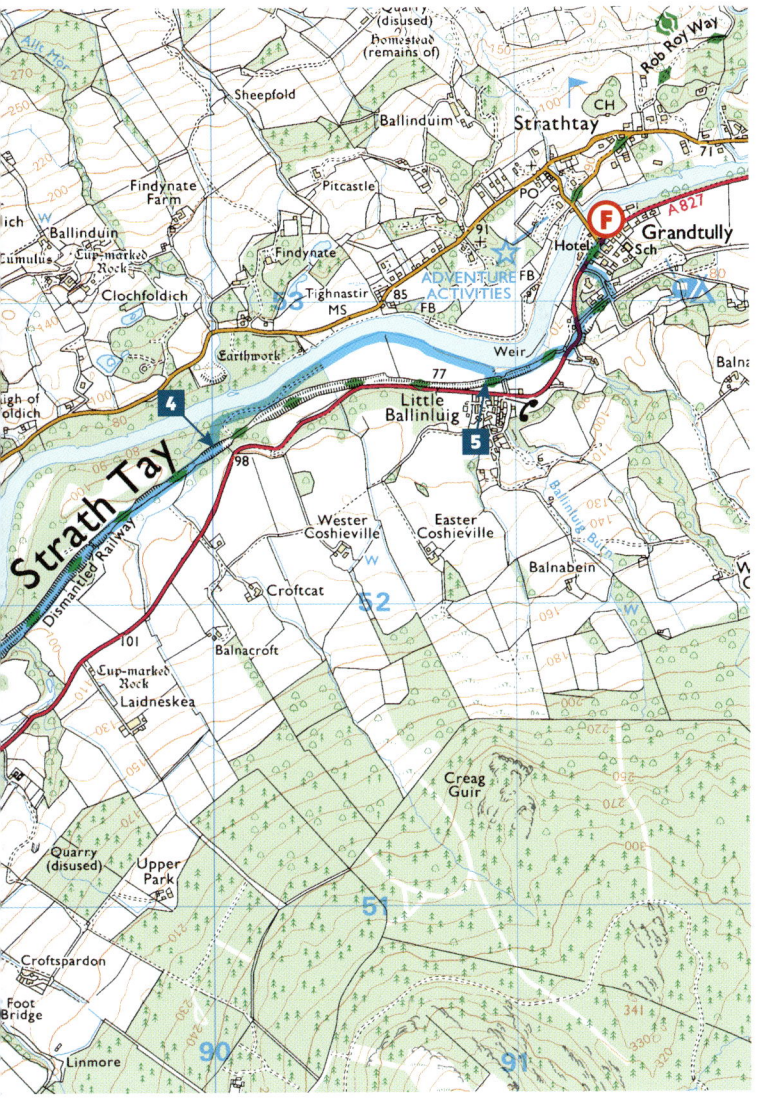

The walk skirts a field with sunflowers

✚ To lengthen
From Grandtully continue along the Rob Roy Way to Pitlochry, adding 7.3km and 320m ascent (2hr 30min).

The Rob Roy Way

Commencing south of Loch Lomond and The Trossachs National Park, the Rob Roy Way travels for 127km to Pitlochry. The trail enters Perthshire by Loch Tay and runs alongside the River Tay to Grandtully, where it forks north to its final destination. It was named and devised from the various hiding locations of the notorious Robert Roy MacGregor (1671–1734), a Jacobite, outlaw and cattle thief. Pardoned by King George I, Rob Roy became a folk hero, immortalised in the anonymous 1723 book *The Highland Rogue*, in the poem 'Rob Roy's Grave' by William Wordsworth, as the title of Berlioz's overture of 1831, and in Sir Walter Scott's 1917 novel *Rob Roy*. The Rob Roy Way became one of Scotland's Great Trails in 2012 (www.scotlandsgreattrails.com).

WALK 12
The Birks of Aberfeldy

Start/finish	*Birks of Aberfeldy car park*
Locate	*///exhale.unwraps.prospers*
Cafes/pubs	*Nearest in Aberfeldy*
Transport	*To Aberfeldy centre (10min from start): bus 24 from Pitlochry changing at stop 'Inn' in Ballinluig for bus 23 or 23X from Dunkeld, several buses from Perth*
Parking	*Birks of Aberfeldy car park (free, PH15 2LD)*
Toilets	*No public toilets on route*

This popular walk among birch, elm, oak and ash trees offers complete immersion in the poetical scenery of Moness Burn and Falls. Although short in distance and straightforward to follow, the route climbs significantly to the highest falls, so take care on any muddy sections, particularly upon descending.

Time 1hr 45min
Distance 3.5km (2.2 miles)
Climb 160m

Possibly the most well-known and beloved of short walks in northern Perthshire, named after Robert Burns's song lyric 'The Birks o'Aberfeldie'

The beautiful Falls of Moness

There are a few benches and comfortable rocks to take a breather

1 Starting at the lower car park, pass another car park, head past the Robert Burns-themed gates, pass information boards and picnic tables, and keep ahead to complete the walk in an anticlockwise direction. At the bench keep right, away from Moness Burn, then ignore steps on the right. Climbing more steeply with impressive drops into the gorge, pass another bench as a wooden barrier appears. Cross over little waterfalls, turn left down stone steps and arrive at the main bridge over the beautiful **Falls of Moness**.

A wooded boardwalk and stairs connect to the bottom of the gorge (photo: Leila Scobie)

2 Across the bridge, the route descends down the other side of the gorge quite steeply, and can be slippery in wet weather. Continue along the path through **Moness Dun Wood** to reach a viewing platform towards the main falls, with Robert Burns's famous words inscribed into the timber. Soon after, spot the little cave with a natural stone seat where Robert Burns penned his song 'The Birks o'Aberfeldie' in August 1787. Continue downhill, passing waterfalls in

WALK 12 – THE BIRKS OF ABERFELDY

succession. After approximately 10min, head down wooden steps and over a boardwalk.

3 After a further few minutes, pass a bench (a statue of a seated Burns will hopefully be returned to the bench). A couple of minutes later, reach the lower banks of the river gorge. Turn left over **Moness Burn** then go right, back to the car parks.

Sitting next to Scotland's beloved national poet (photo: Leila Scobie)

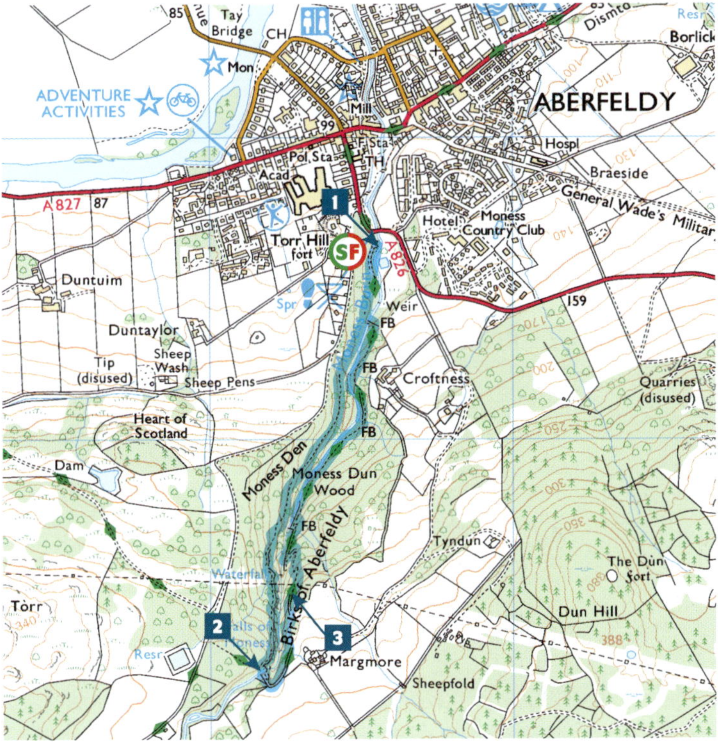

Robert Burns

Several tokens to Robert Burns are passed on this walk

As Scotland's beloved national poet, Robert Burns (1759–1796) is celebrated across the world for 'Auld Lang Syne', sung at Hogmanay (31 December). In Scotland, 'Burns Suppers' are held annually around his birthday on 25 January in his honour. Burns visited Perthshire during his Highland tour in 1787. The woodlands and wealth of falls of Moness Burn inspired his song lyric written in Old Scots as an ode to the 'birks' ('birch trees' in Gaelic) along this spectacular gorge in Aberfeldy.

*'Bonie lassie, will ye go,
Will ye go, will ye go,
Bonie lassie, will ye go
To the birks of Aberfeldie!'*

Extract from 'The Birks o'Aberfeldie' by Robert Burns

Plaque commemorating Robert Burns's 1787 song 'The Birks O'Aberfeldie'

WALK 13
Aberfeldy bridges, St David's Well and Castle Menzies

Time 2hr 30min
Distance 6.9km (4.3 miles)
Climb 170m

An entertaining teetering bridge is succeeded by a mystical well, a large castle, and the most elegant of Perthshire's 18th-century military bridges

Start/finish	The Birks Cinema, Aberfeldy
Locate	///poetic.should.fizzy
Cafes/pubs	Several in Aberfeldy
Transport	Bus 24 from Pitlochry changing at stop 'Inn' in Ballinluig for bus 23 or 23X from Dunkeld, several buses from Perth
Parking	Residential side streets off high street, car parks at Birks of Aberfeldy (free, PH15 2LD) and Moness Terrace (free, PH15 2AF)
Toilets	The Birks Cinema in Aberfeldy and at Castle Menzies

A preamble through Aberfeldy's groomed golf course leads to an exciting, modern bridge over the Tay before rambling to a mystical well in delightful Weem Forest on narrower paths with some rocky steps along the way. The walk culminates with historical Castle Menzies, the elegant Tay Bridge, and a monument dedicated to the Black Watch Regiment. Allow extra time for the castle visit.

The 18th-century Tay Bridge

SHORT WALKS PERTHSHIRE NORTH

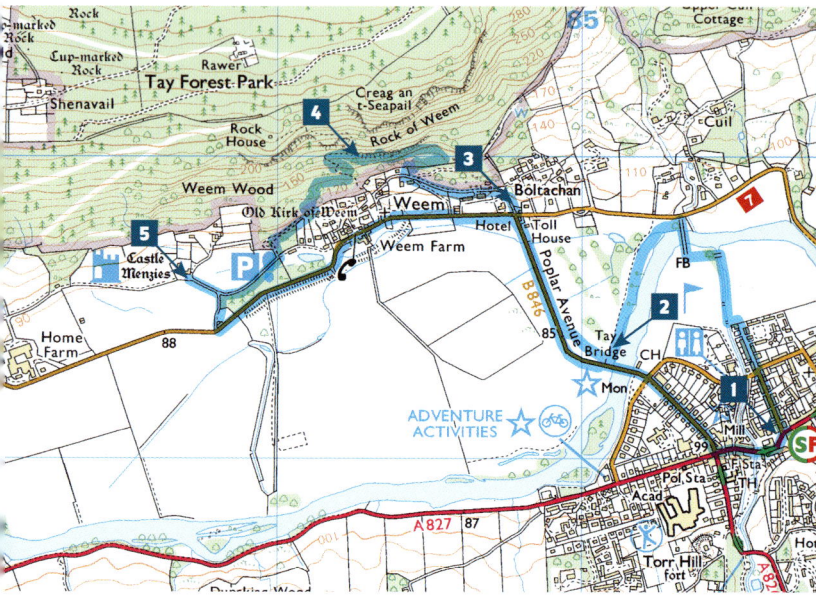

1 Go down Tayside Terrace adjacent to the cinema. Upon entering the **golf course**, keep to the signs and along Moness Burn down to the **River Tay**. Turn left, cross the modern swaying footbridge over the river, then take the path closest to your left. The excitingly fun bridge was designed by the University of Dundee in 1992. It was the world's first all-plastic footbridge and remains the longest one of its kind globally. Pass benches with views towards Tay Bridge (crossed on the return route) and, at the next crossroads of paths, keep to the one closest to the river again.

2 Just before **Tay Bridge**, turn right through the field, left through a car park then right and join the pavement along the B846 towards Weem to reach a junction where the road makes a sharp left turn.

> The 18th-century Tay Bridge is considered one of the most elegant and least military in style of the 40 bridges ordered by General Wade as part of his network of roads constructed after the 1715 Jacobite risings.

WALK 13 – ABERFELDY BRIDGES, ST DAVID'S WELL AND CASTLE MENZIES

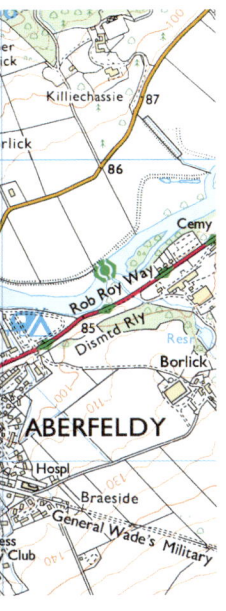

Weem Wood is a medley of conifers and colourful deciduous trees

3 Following a sign for 'Glassie Circular' ahead, take the right-hand uphill gravel track among houses. Pass signposts, keep ahead, then, at the next junction, turn right uphill and right again at the next junction, soon spotting a wooden post marked with red as your path makes a hairpin bend to the left. Head up wooden steps with wooden barriers towards the bigger

First lodging St Cuthbert, this pool amongst the rocky bluffs sheltered David of Menzies in the 15th century

rock faces of the **Rock of Weem**. As you approach St David's Well and the modern Celtic-inspired cross, look out for carvings on rocks and trees relating to the forest's stories. The well and cross mark the spot where the hermits St Cuthbert (7th century) and David of Menzies (15th century) lived their lives of religious solitude. 'Weem' stems from the Gaelic *uaimh* for 'cave'.

4 On leaving the well, continue on the well-trodden path, head down some steps, and promptly detour right to a viewpoint before returning to the path and down steps. Three junctions appear in succession: go right at the first, left at the second and right at the last one, arriving at a car park. Cross over it and turn right, with **Castle Menzies** directly ahead, noting a left-hand track that you will take after exploring the castle.

> **Sumptuous Castle Menzies (www. castlemenzies.org) was built in 1571 by James Menzies and was rescued by the Clan Menzies Society from its derelict state in the 1960s. It houses a fantastic museum. Enquire here about visiting Weem's Old Parish Kirk (1609), one of Scotland's few remaining churches from the early 17th century.**

5 From the castle, return to the track noted earlier, turn right onto it and reach the B846. Turn left along its pavement, swiftly arriving in the village of **Weem**. Pass the old church, then the new church. Find the paths that run parallel to the road keeping you off

Castle Menzies

Aberfeldy's pristine golf course

it: first on the left then on the right. The B846 takes you back to **Aberfeldy**. This time, cross the Tay Bridge and spot the Black Watch Monument on the riverbank to your right. Find yourself on the main street in town and turn left to the cinema.

Founded in Aberfeldy in 1739, the Black Watch Regiment was one of six armies invigilating the Highlands. The cairn-shaped memorial was sculpted in 1887, although the climbing soldier was added after lightning split the boulder in 1910.

– To shorten

From the town centre, go directly to the historic Tay Bridge, saving about 15min.

Aberfeldy

Aberfeldy prospered from its origins as a village in 1739, owing to its strategic position on the crossing of the Tay, carrying General Wade's military road from Crieff to Dalnacardoch. In fact, the town's name stems from both the Pictish word *aber* for 'confluence' and the Gaelic *peallaidh*, referring to a Celtic water-spirit feared in local traditions up until the 19th century. With a bustling collection of restaurants, cafes and shops, life revolves around The Square (1806), and the nearby Art Deco style cinema was inaugurated in 1939. Both the old meal and tweed mills used to operate from Moness Burn in the 19th century.

Above the Falls of Acharn the walk goes through countryside with fantastic views

WALK 14
The Falls of Acharn

Start/finish	*Falls of Acharn car park on Queen's Drive, Acharn*
Locate	*///yacht.variances.fairway*
Cafes/pubs	*None on route*
Transport	*Buses 893, 91 and 91A from Kenmore (weekdays only)*
Parking	*Designated parking on Queen's Drive, Acharn (free, PH15 2HS)*
Toilets	*No public toilets on route*

Time 2hr 30min
Distance 5.5km (3.4 miles)
Climb 330m

A mysterious old viewpoint over roaring waterfalls before an uphill walk to a vantage point reveals the high peaks around Loch Tay

This well-signed route ascends on a wide track with some loose stones underfoot to the Hermit's Cave, which gazes across the gorge to the impressive 73m-tall Falls of Acharn. From there it continues up Queen's Drive, with extensive panoramas, to visit a Bronze Age stone circle. It then descends on the other side of Acharn Burn on potentially muddy paths. This walk is part of the Rob Roy Way (see Walk 11).

The signage on this walk is excellent

1 Start at the designated car parking spot just off National Cycle Route 7 (eastern banks of Loch Tay) on Queen's Drive in **Acharn**. Head up the wide track alongside Acharn Burn, ascending steeply for about 15min. Turn left by the grassy mound, following the sign for the Hermit's Cave. Halfway through the dark tunnel, take the left-hand passage to the viewpoint looking across to the mighty **Falls of Acharn**, then leave the cave through the other end.

> The man-made Hermit's Cave was built in the 1760s to thrill the adventure-seeking guests of Taymouth Castle. To add to the macabre dungeon-like tunnel, the walls were decorated with moss and taxidermy animals, and the stone parapets were laid with hides. It even held a library and furniture.

2 Turn left along the track (soon passing an option to shortcut back to Acharn by heading left and over a wooden bridge and boardwalk) and reach the top of the ravine.

3 Cross the ravine (although it isn't obvious you have done so until you start descending along the other side of it at Waypoint 6) and come to a junction with many signs. Head left to return directly to Acharn instead of visiting the stone circle. To continue the walk, carry on along **Queen's Drive** farm track, now on flatter

The short but very dark tunnel known as the Hermit's Cave

WALK 14 – THE FALLS OF ACHARN

terrain, to reach a crossroads at the end of the track.

As you go, look out towards Loch Tay, the Lawers mountain range to the south-west, the northern Grampian mountains, and even loch-side Kenmore to the north-west. Ben Lawers, the tallest peak visible south-west across Loch Tay, is Scotland's – and the UK's – ninth highest mountain.

4 At the crossroads, turn right up a grassy track through more meadows. After a gate in the drystone wall, you will find the **stone circle** in the field on the right.

> Only four stones now stand while a further three lie flat. It used to be called the 'Greenland Stone Circle', a nod to the surrounding green pastures. The name Acharn is of Gaelic origin, meaning 'cairn field', and likely refers to this field of stones above the hamlet.

5 Return the same way to the junction with many signs at the top of the falls.

6 Follow signs for Acharn. Descend beside Acharn Burn on a dirt path through woods, with some wooden steps helping with muddy sections. Promptly pass the wooden bridge and boardwalk on the left, then a clearing looking across the gorge towards the Hermit's Cave. The falls can be heard crashing below yet are not visible. About 5min later, pass by a ruin and a stone building, before arriving back in **Acharn**. Turn left along the main road by the bus stop, cross over the burn and reach the car park.

> **— To shorten**
> Skip the additional 1hr hike up to the stone circle and head directly down the ravine from Waypoint 6.

Views of the Lawers range along farm tracks above Acharn

WALK 14 – THE FALLS OF ACHARN

A majestic ash tree towers above Loch Tay

Dorothy Wordsworth's 1803 trip

Acharn drew many prestigious 19th-century visitors, including Queen Victoria and John Mendelssohn, but it was Dorothy Wordsworth's visit with her poet brother, William, that evokes how landscapes were dramatised at the time. Seeking contemplation in the romantic settings of Perthshire, her frank *Recollections of a Tour Made in Scotland* disclose that she was not always endeared to the 18th-century architecture, describing both Taymouth Castle and Aberfeldy's Tay Bridge as 'ugly'. Yet, she was enthralled by the 'magic', dizziness and vitality of both the Acharn and Dunkeld hermitages.

Entrance to 19th-century Taymouth Castle and grounds

WALK 15
Drummond Hill and Black Rock Viewpoint

Time 2hr 30min
Distance 8.8km (5.5 miles)
Climb 320m

Wide tracks through mature beech forest lead to outstanding views above Loch Tay and Kenmore

Start/finish	*Kenmore Beach*
Locate	*///pure.maternal.unstated*
Cafes/pubs	*In Kenmore*
Transport	*Buses 91 and 91A from Aberfeldy, and 893 from Killin*
Parking	*Kenmore Beach car park (free, PH15 2HF) or Kenmore Visitor Centre (free)*
Toilets	*Kenmore Visitor Centre*

This walk undulates along wide tracks, through the beech and larch forest of Drummond Hill, home to the capercaillie. It climbs significantly to reach a fantastic viewpoint over Loch Tay and pretty Kenmore. On the descent, the paths may be muddy and slippery. It is very well-signed, following wooden posts with a red (Taymouth Trail) and/or blue (Black Rock Trail) strip.

This walk follows a combination of the blue and red waymarked trails

Views from Kenmore's beach stretch to the Lawers mountain range

1 At Kenmore Beach car park, step onto the main road (A827). With your back to Loch Tay, turn left uphill through the village and pass the gates to Taymouth Castle grounds. Pass the Kenmore Hotel, Kenmore's grocery shop and the church, and cross over the **River Tay** on the pretty bridge.

> The scenic five-arch bridge over the Tay at Kenmore was constructed in 1774 with £1000 from Scotland's Highland Annexed Estates. Annexed to the Crown, funds from the annexed estates helped improve Highland living conditions.

Proceed past the visitor centre and turn immediately right, following the forestry sign for Drummond Hill. After this road bends right, take a grassy path on the left to shortcut up to the Drummond Hill car park, although the road also reaches it.

2 At the information board, get acquainted with your upcoming route. Go left on the wide track gradually uphill. After about 5min, head right and uphill at the red and blue striped post to reach a crossroads of tracks. Note that after the viewpoint you will retrace your steps to this crossroads.

> Drummond Hill's woods, one of the UK Forestry Commission's first ever purchases, were planted during an extensive 16th-century reforestation project by the Laird of Breadalbane. The conifers are home to the rare capercaillie, a type of grouse only found in Scotland in the UK.

3 Go left at the crossroads, following the green sign for the viewpoint, now

A fine view over Kenmore and Loch Tay through beech and giant conifers

> ⓘ *Once extinct in the UK, the capercaillie, Europe's largest grouse, was reintroduced on Drummond Hill in 1837.*

only on the blue trail. Promptly take a left-hand path which brings you to **Black Rock Viewpoint** over Loch Tay and Kenmore. Sinuous Loch Tay is Scotland's sixth largest loch, stretching for 25.8km. The River Tay passes through the loch on its 188km-journey to the Firth of Tay in Dundee.

4 Return the same way to the crossroads of tracks. Once there, keep straight and downhill, now only on the red trail. Reach another crossroads 15min later.

The red Taymouth Trail borrows its name from the spectacular powerhouse that is the mock-gothic Taymouth Castle. It was built between 1802 and 1842 by the Campbells of Breadalbane, who owned all of Kenmore parish until 1920.

5 Turn right, following the red waymark, and immediately right again onto the closest right-hand path, often muddy underfoot. Meander down through denser woodland for 720m.

6 Once down the hill, turn right onto the wide track, then left onto the track from the start of the walk and retrace your steps through the village back to the car park.

WALK 15 – DRUMMOND HILL AND BLACK ROCK VIEWPOINT

− To shorten
Head up to the viewpoint and back down the same way, totalling 6.4km (1hr 30min).

+ To lengthen
Complete the grey Caisteal MacTuat Hal Trail, giving a walk of 9.4km (3hr).

The Kenmore Hotel: one of Scotland's oldest inns

Originally the parish minister's manse, the Kenmore Hotel (due to reopen in 2026) was a public house from the 16th century, then established as a hotel after the bridge facilitated access. Amongst its visitors, Oliver Cromwell and his soldiers dined here as they pursued the Earl of Montrose; Robert Burns visited the hotel and his verses are pencilled upon the breast of the parlour fireplace; siblings Dorothy and William Wordsworth visited in 1803; and Queen Victoria and Prince Albert honeymooned here.

Look out for three animal-themed stones along the route

USEFUL INFORMATION

Tourism bodies

Forestry and Land Scotland
https://forestryandland.gov.scot

Highland Perthshire Tourism
www.highlandperthshire.org

Historic Environment Scotland
www.historicenvironment.scot

National Trust for Scotland
www.nts.org.uk

Perth and Kinross Council
www.pkc.gov.uk/paths

Perth and Kinross Countryside Trust
www.pkct.org

Visit Scotland
www.visitscotland.com/places-to-go/perthshire

Tourist information

Aberfeldy and Kenmore Information Centre
www.visitaberfeldy.co.uk

Blair Castle
https://atholl-estates.co.uk

Castle Menzies
www.castlemenzies.org

Dunkeld Community Archive
www.historicdunkeld.org.uk

Taymouth Castle
https://welcometotaymouth.com

Informative websites

Dunkeld and Birnam
www.dunkeldandbirnam.org.uk

Kinloch Rannoch
www.kinlochrannoch.com

Visitors to autumnal Perthshire will delight in the array of colours

USEFUL INFORMATION

Loch Rannoch and the River Tummel
https://rannochandtummel.co.uk

Pitlochry
https://pitlochry-scotland.co.uk

Travel

Rail
www.scotrail.co.uk

Coaches
www.citylink.co.uk and
https://uk.megabus.com

Local bus routes
www.pkc.gov.uk/article/14961/
Highland-Perthshire-and-Stanley-
area-timetables

National Cycle Network
www.sustrans.org.uk/
national-cycle-network

Bibliography

Wild Flowers of Perthshire by Peter and Margaret Cramb (P & M Cramb, 2000)

The Buildings of Scotland: Perth and Kinross by John Gifford (Yale University Press, 2007)

Perth and Kinross: An illustrated architectural guide by Nick Haynes (The Rutland Press, 2000)

The Perthshire Book by Donald Omand (Birlinn Limited, 1999)

Checklist of the Plants of Perthshire by RAH Smith, NF Stewart, NW Taylor and RE Thomas (Perthshire Society of Natural Science, 1992)

© Nicole Bukaty 2025
First edition 2025
ISBN: 978 1 78631 252 5
eISBN: 978 1 78765 216 3

Printed in Singapore by KHL Printing on responsibly sourced paper.
A catalogue record for this book is available from the British Library.
All photographs are by the author unless otherwise stated.
Cover illustration of The Atholl Palace Hotel by Clare Crooke.

© Crown copyright and database rights 2025 OS AC0000810376

Cicerone's EU representative for GPSR compliance is Easy Access System Europe, Mustamäe tee 50, 10621 Tallinn, Estonia. Email gpsr.requests@easproject.com.

CICERONE

Cicerone Press, Juniper House, Murley Moss, Oxenholme Road,
Kendal, Cumbria, LA9 7RL

www.cicerone.co.uk

Updates to this Guide

While every effort is made to ensure the accuracy of guidebooks as they go to print, changes can occur during the lifetime of an edition. Any updates that we know of for this guide will be on the Cicerone website (www.cicerone.co.uk/1252/updates), so please check before planning your trip. We also advise that you check information about transport, accommodation and shops locally. Even rights of way can be altered over time. We are always grateful for information about any discrepancies between a guidebook and the facts on the ground, sent by email to updates@cicerone.co.uk.

Register your book: To sign up to receive free updates, special offers and GPX files where available, create a Cicerone account and register your purchase via the 'My Account' tab at www.cicerone.co.uk.